Project for the Panama Canal

Lindon Wallace Bates

INDEX

PLANS AND DIAGRAMS

INTRODUCTION.

The Panama Canal is an undertaking of the vastest meaning to America, commercially and nationally. Its construction should be so correct as to leave nothing for present regret or future challenge.

It becomes in some measure the duty of every engineer who cherishes his ideal for this great public work to break his silence and reserve if he perceives that in any vital degree or at any remediable point the Canal seems failing of the highest that it can achieve.

No one knows more intimately the elements, no one knows more profoundly the difficulties, inherent in this vast problem, than the eminent men, French and American, who, from the inception in 1879 all the way to to-day, have studied and planned by the best in them to solve its perplexities. Let praise go to them unstinted, for this is their smallest due.

Believing profoundly, though reluctantly, that the announced methods of solution are not such as to secure to the American people the best, the safest and the most enduring Canal, the writer feels that he would be faithless to his citizenship did he not state so. Knowing further that there exists a more scientific method, it has become his duty, as well as his privilege, to set it forth.

ISTHMUS OF PANAMA.

FACTORS AND CONDITIONS.

The physical factors existing and the conditions appertaining to the Isthmus of Panama appear in the many published Official Reports of the various Isthmian Commissions appointed by the United States; in the debates of Congress: in the studies of the Comité Technique of the old and new Panama Companies: in the numerous scientific articles which have been contributed to the Engineering Press, notably those by Gen. H. L. Abbot, by the late George Morrison, by members of the existing Commission, and by the Minister to Panama.

In view of the copious available authoritative literature, it is deemed unnecessary to epitomize or recapitulate here those elements or to present, except incidentally, the results of the most recent surveys, borings, and explorations, on which are based serious commitments looking toward a Sea-Level Canal with Tunnel Diversions of the Chagres River.

CHARACTER AND DESCRIPTION OF THE PRESENT FAVORED PROJECTS.

I. Project of the Comité Technique. This plan is set forth in the Official Report of the last Commission (Pages 85-86). It has been ardently advocated, and particularly by Gen. H. L. Abbot, long associated with the French companies as one of their consulting engineers.

The summit level of this scheme is 62.5 feet mean height above sea level. It is to be created by a dam at Bohio, supplemented by one at Alhajuela to assure an adequate water supply for lockage, evaporation, seepage and percolation. The Gigantè Spillway is likewise an integral feature.

II. Isthmian Commission Project of 1901. This, the 85-foot Summit Level Plan, is fully described in the same Official Report (Pages 91 to 99). It was the basis of the treaty with the Republic of Panama and of the purchase from the new Canal Company in 1904. The Gigantè Spillway is here also an essential feature.

III. 30-Foot Summit Level Project. Recently a Two-Lock, 30-foot level plan has been mooted, but no details have yet been set forth. It involves probably a dam and lock on the Atlantic side at Bohio, as well as a lock near Pedro Miguel or Miraflores close to the Pacific end, and also dam provisions similar to those of the French project. The topography of the Bohio Lake Basin precludes any surface spillway and some other provision is indispensable.

An alternative "30-foot level" plan might propose that the summit level be between a lock at Obispo and one between Miraflores and Pedro Miguel. This level would involve a feeding reservoir behind a Gamboa or Alhajuela Dam and auxiliary works at a level hardly compatible with the main regulation offices of the great dam.

IV. Sea-Level Project. This historically disastrous, much discussed, much sought and much idealized scheme has recently been resuscitated. It now pro poses a canal at mean ocean-level with a tide lock at Miraflores, a gigantic dam at Gamboa creating a large lake, and long "Diversion Tunnels (or several up-river dams and several tunnels) to carry the impounded waters of the Upper Chagres" through the broken volcanic formations which encircle its watershed, and down valleys into the Pacific Ocean or Caribbean Sea.

The Tunnel idea was considered by the French Engineers and was rejected, not because their examination did not reveal sites, but because the tunnels were too hazardous an expedient technically and financially.

REMARKS.

As thirty to thirty-three feet is rightly recognized as the safe limit of lift for a great ship-lock, the first three projects mentioned naturally embody the Six-Lock, the Four-Lock and the Two-Lock systems in relation to Bohio, Gamboa and Alhajuela Lake Solutions. All these schemes include high impounded lakes of great depth, area and volume subject to torrential additions to their already imposing levels. It is one thing, and a simple thing, to catch and regulate a Chagres deluge by adequate and empty lake basins, but it is quite another venture to receive it in a high, full lake where it can jeopardize an investment of $300,000,000, and the commerce of a hemisphere. The Sea-Level Plan brings the Atlantic to Miraflores, where a tide-gate is located.

The tide-gate is necessary in each instance because of the difference in the tidal régime of the two ocean terminals, as to which the following table is pertinent:

TIDES AT PANAMA.

	At Naos Island	At La Boca.
High water at full and change of moon	III h 16 m	III h 16 m
Low water at full and change of moon	IX " 34 "	IX " 27 "
Corrected establishment for high water	III " 02 "	II " 59 "
Corrected establishment for low water	IX " 12 "	IX " 06 "
Mean height of high water at spring tide above plane of reference	14.90 ft.	15.90 ft.
Mean height of low water at spring tide below plane of reference	2.08 "	4.12 "

	At Naos Island	At La Boca
Mean height of high water neap tides above plane of reference.............................	10.35 ft.	10.40 ft.
Mean height of low water at neap tide above plane of reference.............................	2.45 "	2.43 "
Mean range of tides.............................	12.85 "	13.47 "
Mean range of spring tides.......................	16.98 "	20.02 "
Mean range of neap tides.......................	7.80 "	7.97 "

(The plane of reference is mean low water level.)

Mean sea-level appears to be about 6.16 to 6.41 feet above the plane of reference, and with respect to mean ocean level the range may be considered between + 10 and —10.

TIDES AT COLON.

Mean Tidal Variations at Colon.....................	1.43 ft.
Maximum Tidal Variations at Colon	2.07 "
Minimum Tidal Variations at Colon.................	0.62 "

LINDON BATES' PROJECT.

This conception is new. It is radically and fundamentally different from all the previous plans and alternative projects which have been published heretofore or are now under consideration. No critical or comparative analysis of the various projects is now made, but the evolution and the character of the new design is first described, with only such references to others as may seem necessary to its understanding.

PRIMARY CONSIDERATIONS.

RELATION OF EARNING POWER TO COST.

The interrelations which exist between the cost of the design definitely adopted and the Canal's future business and profit as a national enterprise are of supreme importance.

Since the Panama Canal is to be used as a highway for the shipping of the world, from which a net tonnage toll is to be collected for each passage, it follows that this work should be treated as a business undertaking and a forecast should be made as to its probable outcome as an enterprise with the federal government as investor.

From this standpoint such forecast becomes imperative, since it defines the permissible capital expenditure.

9

COST OF CANAL.

To Construction..........................	$144,222,358	
To Purchase P. C. Co......................	40,000,000	
To Purchase Zone Strip....................	10,000,000	
To Purchase Outstanding Ry. Bonds........	3,000,000	$197,222,358
Total Cost (Round).............................		$197,000,000

PRESENT INVESTMENT.

To Purchase Zone Strip....................	$10,000,000	
To Purchase P. C. Co......................	40,000,000	50,000,000
Difference to be spent in 10 years		147,000,000

CAPITAL TO BE PROVIDED.

To Total Cost............................	$197,000,000	
To Interest 10 years Const. period 2 per cent. 10 years, $50,000,000....................	10,000,000	
2 per cent. 5 years, $147,000,000..............	14,700,000	
To Deficit operation (1915–16–17).............	12,000,000	
Total		$233,700,000

EARNING AND EXPENSES 1915–16–17.

EARNINGS.

The Commission Report of 1901 gives the probable available canal tonnage for 1914 as 6,843,805 tons. With the decade increment of 25.1 per cent. therein accepted, the available tonnage in 1917 will amount to 7,279,000 net tons, all of which at this time—it is assumed—will pass through the Canal. The tonnage for 1915–16, which represents the beginning of operation, will naturally be less.

The actual increase in traffic resulting from the opening of the Canal is taken to begin in 1917.

The Commission Report of 1901 adopted 62½ per cent. as rate of tonnage increase for the first decade (after beginning of traffic) and derived this by taking 50 per cent. of the tonnage increase of the Suez Canal from 1880 to 1890. In 1880 the total net tonnage of the Suez Canal was about 3,000,000 tons, but the Panama Canal (it is considered) will begin operation in 1917 with the above

7,000,000 tons, and for this reason, the decade 1893-1903 of Suez operation, which begins with the above 7,600,000 tons, provides a better analogy as to character and quantity of traffic than the 1880-90 decade. The 1893-1903 decade shows an average increment of 45 per cent. beginning with 7,645,000 tons and this figure is used for the 1917-1927 decade of Panama Canal.

The Suez and Panama Canals will also be competitors for a large amount of tonnage and this condition may reduce the above rate of tonnage increase. At the accepted rate of $1.00 per net ton the earnings become

1915 (assumed)...................................	$1,000,000
1916 (assumed)...................................	5,000,000
1917 from above discussion...................	7,279,000

OPERATING EXPENSES.

FIXED CHARGES—PER YEAR.

$233,700,000. Capital to be provided by issuance of 2 per cent. bonds or use of Treasury Surplus on which at least 2 per cent. should be calculated. Interest at 2 per cent...............	$4,674,000	
Sinking Fund and Extraordinary Contingencies ¾ per cent......	1,752,750	
OPERATION.		
By Report of Commission 1901 ...	2,000,000	
Total		$8,426,750

Deficit 1915....................	$7,426,750	
1916....................	3,426,750	
1917....................	1,147,750	
Provided for in Capital....................		$12,001,250

FOR 1918, FIRST YEAR OF FULL OPERATION.

With 45 per cent. per decade increase in traffic, The Income becomes..........................	$7,606,555	
Total Operating Expenses..	8,426,750	
Deficit		$820,195

Time, until total operating expenses equal income at 45 per cent. decade rate beginning 1917, is 2.5 years from 1918 or 5½ years after opening of Canal

TABLES.

The results of above steps for the Summit Levels of 85 ft., 60 ft., 30 ft. and Sea-Level Projects are tabulated below.

CONSTRUCTION.

	Total cost (construction cost plus $53,000,000).	Interest during 10 year construction period.	Deficit for opening years of operation, 1915-16-17.	Total capital required.
85 ft.	$197,000,000	$24,700,000	$12,000,000	$233,700,000
60 ft.	231,013,000	28,101,300	15,385,700	274,500,000
30 ft.	247,213,000	29,721,300	16,965,700	293,900,000
S.-Level.	283,500,000	33,350,000	20,550,000	337,400,000

OPERATION.

	Interest 2% per annum on total capital.	Sinking fund and extraordinary contingencies at ¾%	Total yearly expenses including $2,000,000 for operation.	Income for 1918 from tonnage at $1.00 net ton.
85 ft.	$4,674,000	$1,752,750	$8,426,750	$7,606,555
60 ft.	5,490,000	2,058,750	9,548,750	7,606,555
30 ft.	5,878,000	2,204,250	10,082,250	7,606,555
S.-Level.	6,748,000	2,530,500	11,278,500	7,606,555

OPERATION.

	Deficit in 1918.	Years after opening: When operation expenses=income.	Income for 1927 from tonnage $1.00 net ton end 1st decade.	Difference between expenses and income for 1927.
85 ft.	$820,195	5.5	10,554,550	2,127,750 Surplus.
60 ft.	1,942,195	8.9	10,554,550	1,005,800 Surplus.
30 ft.	2,475,695	11.6	10,554,550	472,300 Surplus.
S.-Level.	3,671,945	Not in decade	10,554,550	723,950 Deficit.

From the above, the effect on the results of increasing the Construction Cost is apparent. For each case $50,000,000 is considered as having been already invested, while the remainder of the Total Construction is to be paid out at a uniform rate during the ten year construction period.

The revenue from tonnage toll at $1.00 per net ton is the only source of income considered.

The fixed charges and operating expenses will remain constant for the scope of these calculations, regardless of the tonnage passing through the Canal.

Increase or decrease in the toll per net ton effects in direct proportion the amount of annual earnings and therefore the amount of the surplus or deficit; and finally the amount of capital that can be advisedly expended in the undertaking.

Following diagram indicates the several results in the table plotted to scale.

A scale for yearly earnings based upon $1.25 per net ton as tonnage toll is also given.

Assuming a total capital outlay of $337,400,000 in ten years to secure a sea level canal with a tunnel from the Chagres Watershed:—

There will be a large annual deficit running for many years.

At tolls of $1.25 per ton this deficit still persists, gradually diminishing as traffic increases.

CONCLUSIONS.

This outlook means that, if possible, consistently with its highest good. no more than 145 millions construction cost should be dedicated to this enterprise by the Government of the United States, in addition to the present investment.

There is nothing which warrants now a sea-level canal requiring $230,500,000 additional, and returning for it a channel too small at any price. There is, however, every warrant in commercial outlook and in military necessity for a canal costing an outlay, aside from interest, of the 145 millions of the money allotted by Congress in the Spooner Act.

The undersigned submits that his projects can be executed for less than this sum, that he has the relations which will enable the whole work to be responsibly undertaken for a definite amount, to be finished in a definite time of eight years, and to be successfully operated and maintained.

RECENT ESTIMATES.

The first definite engineering plans for the construction of the Panama Canal have just been made public.

The principal recommendations are summed up in this resolution:

"That this committee approve and recommend for adoption by the commission a plan for a sea-level canal, with a bottom width of 150 feet and a minimum depth of water of 35 feet and with twin tidal locks at Miraflores, whose usable dimensions shall be 1,000 feet long and 100 feet wide, at a total estimated cost of $230,500,000.

"Such estimate includes an allowance for administration, engineering, sanitation and contingencies, amounting to $38,450,000, but without allowance for interest during construction, expense of zone government and collateral costs, and water supply, sewers or paving of Panama or Colon, which last items are to be repaid by the inhabitants of those cities."

The committee estimates that a sea level canal can be completed within from ten to twelve years from the present time.

The committee decided that under no circumstances should the surface of the canal be more than sixty feet above the sea, and estimates that at this level the cost would be $178,013,406. A thirty-foot level is estimated to cost $194,213,406.

PRISM DIMENSIONS.

Primarily the Panama Canal is desired as an aid to navigation. As such it must technically serve the peace and war vessels of to-day and those of at least the next generation. It is not enough that this costly waterway shall admit the passage of ships simply; it must make practical their *safe* transit. The dimensions, therefore, of the ships to be served and of the passage to be traversed become of vital and primary importance, entirely aside from problems of drainage and of excavation volume.

What are the minimum dimensions which will enable the largest merchant or naval vessels of—say—forty years hence, to traverse in security the narrow straight reaches or to negotiate the curves of the canal at a safe steering speed, and what is that speed? No first real effort has been made anywhere to determine these fundamental questions in their relation to even the largest vessels of to-day.

The water section planned in 1901 for the Culebra division is too small and is of the wrong shape. Its channel was designed 150 feet wide at the bottom and only 164 feet at the water surface for some seven or eight miles. A "Deutschland" or a "Baltic," for instance, could not safely negotiate it, as she could not maintain steerage way and avoid sheering against the masonry walls first one side and then the other. Yet despite the facts involved, we have this month an authoritative announcement:

The Engineering Committee of the present Commission has just favorably reported a sea-level project. It proposes a waterway only thirty-five feet deep, at a further outlay of $230,500,000. The following language is used:

"The advantages of a sea-level canal across the Isthmus are most obvious. It would be a waterway with no restriction to navigation, and which could be easily enlarged by widening or deepening at any time in the future, to accommodate an increased traffic, without any inconvenience to the shipping using it,

14

whereas a lock canal is in reality a permanent restriction to the volume of traffic and size of ships that use it. Although it is possible to design and construct locks adapted to the future transformation to a sea-level canal, that transformation cannot be made without serious inconvenience to navigation and at a cost so great as to be excessive."

To such premises the writer does not subscribe. A long, narrow waterway having a section of only 7,150 square feet in "firm earth," and far less in the Culebra division, cannot be either so safely or so quickly traversed by large craft as a canal with lake navigation and locks.

Restricted underwater sections restrict navigation and endanger vessels.

Such a sea-level channel cannot "be easily widened and deepened without any inconvenience to the shipping using it." To deepen such a canal the five feet necessary to accommodate the vessels of even 1917 involves the excavation of vast quantities from the bottom and slopes in which the spoil must be mostly moved long distances longitudinally.

A two-lock canal, if the locks be suited to taking 1,000-foot vessels, is not a permanent restriction to the volume of traffic. More ships can be put through and at an average higher rate of speed than in the sea-level channel, whose dimensions are permanently confined and fixed from the outset by the tremendous cost of further enlargement and the inevitable annual deficits which such outlay entails.

A year has passed and the investigation imperative to reaching a safe conclusion as to dimensions has not even been started. The observations of the writer and studies based upon extensive experiences in connection with many canals lead him to the conviction that from the standpoint of the Science of Navigation:

1st. The basis of speed in the most restricted channel tangents should be set at 5 knots per hour.

2d. The underwater slope should rarely be steeper than 2.5 to 1. This is not because of the geological formation, but because to steer safely the water divided and displaced by a steadily advancing vessel must readily reach the void astern. In certain soft underwater strata this slope of course may best be 3 or 4 to 1 or even flatter. Surface width is a prerequisite for safe steering.

3d. The ruling depth for the ships of ten years hence should be at least 40 ft.

4th. The bottom width should be at least 150 ft.

The above factors give a water surface width of 350 ft. These dimensions mean a minimum water section of 10,000 sq. ft. in tangents. If one takes the steepest slope in the Suez 2 to 1 at El-Guisr, he has 8,000 sq. ft. as an irreducible minimum at the narrowest point in the canal.

As evidenced by the constantly increasing size of vessels, one may expect to see even within a decade steamers 1,000 ft. long and 100 ft. beam, drawing 40 ft. of water. We are already to leviathans 780 ft. long and of 88 ft. beam—the new Cunarders. (Vide Diagram.) The business of the Pacific will be done in ships of the largest size. Battleships will not be so long, but they will be as wide as the 1,000 ft. steamers. Such craft may need for safety a canal 50 ft. wider than even this new proposal and 10 feet deeper.

Though actually correct minimum dimensions and speeds on tangents and curves therefore remain to be finally determined, yet, for the purposes of this presentation a minimum water section of 8,000 sq. ft. at the initial reaches from the Obispo Basin is taken as the smallest allowable starting point of calculations, and the writer makes full reserves.

Slopes above water will naturally be determined by the formation, having regard for stability and weathering. The slopes of the Culebra Section above water will vary from 1¼ to 2 to 1 according to the ground, and must be properly terraced, tunnelled, and drained.

The wider the section at the water surface the better can ships be controlled. It follows that the longer lake navigation of the canal can be made, the safer it will be for shipping.

One of the fundamental objections to a sea-level canal at Panama is the fact that such a channel must be fatally narrow unless the quantities excavated are to be too appalling to contemplate.

A vessel draws more in a fresh than in a salt water channel. Canal dimensions are ordinarily such that a large vessel must push a great swell of water which cannot get astern or to one side. Thus it happens that the large vessels literally settle by the stern sometimes several feet. Hence security demands an adequate excess of canal depth over loaded draft. Vessels plying around the Cape of Good Hope to Australia are permitted by their Plimsoll marks to load 33 or 34 feet, which becomes 34 or 35 feet in fresh water, and a margin of five feet is not too great even for the present requirements.

DIMENSIONS IN CULEBRA SECTION.

The great depth of the Culebra Section makes a berm too expensive, and the only recourse is to select a form of section demanded by vessels and rates of slope under and above water which will be permanent, and then make the sides proof against erosive currents induced in the transit of large ships.

The minimum sectional area should be not less than 8,000 sq. ft. If then a batter of 1 in 4 is given to the walls, there will have to be a channel bottom width of 190 feet, and a surface width of 210 feet. With such a shape of section, fenders along the sides will certainly be advisable to prevent the enormous sheering blows which a great vessel is liable to strike at any moment that her bow gets to one side of the canal's axis and upsets the equilibrium of forces. If the bottom width is 160 feet and the underwater slopes 1 to 1, we have a surface width of 240 feet which, while far from ideal, is much fitter to negotiate, although it means 15 ft. more slicing along the imposing terraces above water. The best navigable dimensions to this cut approximate probably the last figures having regard to the vast increase of excavation which greater width at water surface involves. (Vide Diagram.)

LAKE SOLUTIONS.

All the projects enumerated contemplate the creating of high, deep and permanent lakes.

FEET.

I { Lake Bohio...................38.5 sq. M. 89/90 deep at Dam.
{ Gigantè Spillway..............

II { Lake Bohio and..............23 sq. M. 57/68.5 deep at Dam.
{ Gigantè Spillway and
{ Alhajuela Lake...............10 sq. M. 130 deep at Dam.

III A { Lake Bohio (very small)........ sq. M. 30 deep at Dam.
{ Lake Gamboa or Alhajuela....16 sq. M. 85 deep at Dam.
{ No spillway—perhaps tunnels

III B { Lake Gamboa or Alhajuela.....16 sq. M. 85 deep at Dam.
{ Obispo Locks
{ Pedro Miguel or }
{ Miraflores Locks }

IV. { Lake Gamboa or several small
{ lakes aggregating...........20 to 30 sq. M. 145 deep at Dam.
{ Diversion Tunnels through Divides.

The Gigantè Spillway of I and II avowedly may discharge 140,000 c. f. per second into a channel parallel to and many feet above the Canal for eight miles from Pena Blanca to below Gatun.

These permanent high-level lakes, the Gigantè Spillway and the Tunnels are very dangerous and as mechanical expedients wholly unnecessary.

Project II, that of the Comité Technique, is the least objectionable.

Project IV, the rejected and revived Mean Sea-Level scheme of de Lesseps, is experimental technically, and extravagant financially. The absence of an acceptable spillway site also condemns No. III. The many locks of No. I are universally deprecated.

Viewing with such well-founded apprehension the high, full lake projects, the Gigantè Spillway and the Tunnel schemes, the writer has felt impelled to show a feasible and reasonable alternative.

17

SUMMIT LEVEL.

A summit division shall extend from the vicinity of Mindi to the vicinity of La Boca. At each end of this Division shall be twin-locks. The waters at the locks shall be regulated to about 20 ft. above mean sea-level, which the writer deems preferable to a lower or a higher plane. At both the Atlantic and Pacific ends low-level lakes shall be formed—by broad suitably constructed banks connecting the hills east and west of Mindi and by a Barrage across the Chagres as indicated.

The northern lake—Lake Chagres—29.5 sq. miles in area and over 11.8 miles long, extends from Mindi to several miles above Bohio. It will incidentally cover all the lower Chagres Swamps except Pena Blanca, which will be flooded to a higher level, as hereafter mentioned.

The other—Lake Panama—about 5.5 miles long, will be similarly formed from Miraflores to La Boca with an area of 7 sq. miles. It will submerge permanently all of the festering swamps around Panama. Each lake will be entered and left by locking, and the level of each will be adequately regulated by a suitably located Insubmergible Under Sluice Barrage. Such a barrage in its latest and most perfect design has demonstrated its complete success working on a scale much vaster than is required and without foundations upon rock.

For alternatives Gatun may be elected as the site of the Atlantic Lock and Barrage, or Miraflores as the location of the Pacific Lock with a Diversion Channel above the lock leading to a Barrage. Such selections would reduce Lake Navigation to 12 miles—the extent of Lake Bohio.

There will be thus created a total of more than 17¼ miles of what for speed and navigation purposes is practically lake navigation between Mindi and Buena Vista—and between Miraflores and La Boca. Tentative locations for the locks, barrages, and levees are shown on the map. Manifestly topographical and geological considerations may modify slightly the actual locations indicated, but the principles, above set forth, will hold. This lake navigation will be nearly six miles longer than that afforded by the Lake Bohio Projects.

Lake Bohio measures 12 miles in length and at the
65.6 foot level covers 23.08 sq. miles.
82.0 foot level covers 36.78 sq. miles.
85.2 foot level covers 38.48 sq. miles.

DISPOSITION AND REGULATION OF RIVERS.

CHAGRES.

LOWER EAST SIDE.

All tributaries of the Chagres on the east side between Mindi and Bohio will flow into the new Lake Chagres.

The western tributaries between the Dam and the Gigantè will also empty into this Lake. The waters of the drainage basin of the Pena Blanca Swamp and the Rio Gigantè will be led to the submerged Agua Clara Swamp.

There will be a wide, impermeable and insubmergible bank between the Canal Channel and the Pena Blanca Swamp. The level of the water in the latter will be raised to $+30$ ft., which will cover its foulness to a depth of $7\frac{1}{2}$ ft. This height will be readily regulated by a spillway in the Channel between the two swamp areas. No appreciable currents in the track of vessels will be produced by the streams entering the east and west sides of the lake.

CENTRAL WEST SIDE.
MOUTH OF CANO TO CULEBRA.

All the tributaries in this section, except the Rio Cano, are small and can be led to the Canal Channel with only the works necessary for insuring that neither silt deposits nor objectionable local currents shall occur at junctions with the Canal Channels.

The Rio Cano has a large watershed, a recorded maximum discharge of 1640 cu. ft. per second, a mean discharge of 335 and a minimum of 17 ft. per second. At a suitable site, as indicated, an Insubmergible Under Sluice Dam shall be built capable of perfectly regulating the discharge of the Cano Basin.

CANAL CHANNEL AND UPPER CHAGRES REGULATION WORKS.
JUNCTION BASIN.

It will be noted on inspection of the map that at Bas Obispo the axis of the Chagres Valley makes a right angle bend, and the Upper Valley lies between Atlantic and Pacific serrated Coast Ridges.

Obispo is almost exactly half-way between the inner ends of the new Lakes "Chagres" and "Panama." The topography admits the excavation of a triangular Junction Basin in form like a railway "Y." Waters entering this Junction Basin (which will likewise be a convenient turning area for large vessels) will naturally flow north to Lake Chagres and the Atlantic, and south to Lake Panama and the Pacific Ocean.

CHAGRES DISCHARGE CHANNELS.

In effect therefore the Chagres will have two discharge channels, both running from the Junction Basin to a large lake, each channel with an initial minimum water section of 8,000 sq. ft., as before mentioned, or 16,000 sq ft. in all. The Commission stated in 1901 that there would be required to pass the Chagres floods without injury a Channel 15,000 sq. ft. in area. (Page 88.) But under this Project there can be no freshets from either the watershed above or below Gamboa.

From the Junction Basin to Lake Chagres and to Lake Panama the water section widths will expand at a small coefficient rate to take care of the Central Valley Drainage which is allowed to enter the channel. Practically the same low velocity of flow at all points can be thus scientifically assured as in the regulation of tidal rivers like the Weser, Scheldt and Brisbane.

CENTRAL EAST SIDE.

The few creeks between Bohio and Obispo will be led into the Canal Channel, each with suitable small auxiliary works, channels, débris-dams, or weirs and aprons to prevent erosion and the carrying of silt.

DAMS.

At Gamboa and at Alhajuela, across the Valley of the Chagres will be built, "Insubmergible Under-Sluice" Dams, as shown in section in plan.

The Gamboa Dam will control, regulate and discharge:

A. The drainage of the Gamboa Basin Watershed, shown on Plan No. 1.

B. The regulated outflow from the Alhajuela Basin.

The Alhajuela Dam will control, regulate and discharge:

A. The drainage of the "Alhajuela Basin," a name bestowed for convenience on the Chagres Watershed above this dam.

The undersluices of these dams will be operated to maintain the determined level of the Obispo Basin, which is the Governor.

In principle there will be permitted the smallest possible accumulation of water behind the two dams, which nevertheless can safely impound 900,000,000 cubic meters, which may be doubled by additional dams higher up river.

A head of a few inches above +20 in the Obispo Basin will give a discharge of 40,000 c. f. per second from the basin, 20,000 c. f. through each outlet, and will occasion a velocity of only 2½ ft. per second, or 1½ knots per hour. This is less than frequently prevails in the Suez Canal between the Little Bitter Lake and Port Tewfik due to the Red Sea tides. Hence the sluices of the Gamboa Dam can be allowed to pass such large volumes of water that under the worst conditions the catchment basins above could not be nearly filled, and they will possess factors of safety against any fresh contingency. There need be no cascade into Obispo Basin from the Gamboa Sluices—and if there were, it could do no harm—being only picturesque.

There will be no great, high, permanent lakes, no tunnels, no experiments. There will be, instead, merely large and, always, nearly empty catchment basins, capable of perfect discharge control, which can be effected without the slightest inconvenience to navigation. The currents in the navigated channels need never exceed 3 ft. per second and normally they will be much less.

The present conception is not then that of a "canal," but of a canalized river with two diverging outlets, each leading to a large, easily controlled lake and discharging, one into the Atlantic, the other into the Pacific.

The Dam designs shown with this Project are substantially those of the Assuan Dam, which has been perfectly successful in impounding 1,065,000,000 cubic meters. It controls and safeguards the Nile, whose flood-discharge is 804,000 second feet or nearly six times the greatest known flood of the Chagres at Bohio. The height of these Dams can be kept down if desired by supplementary Dams on the main tributaries above Alhajuela.

WATER SUPPLY AND CONTROL

It will be observed that the minimum daily discharge of the Chagres Watershed affords an ample supply of water for lockage, seepage, evaporation and other losses, between Gamboa and the two oceans. On account of the low head, ground seepage will be everywhere immaterial.

By manipulating their sluices the levels of Lakes Chagres and Panama can be raised and lowered. They can be reduced to a sea-level plane or even below. The ruling depth, on the other hand, can be increased to some 45 ft. without a cubic yard of dredging or other material expense and without impairing the safety or efficiency of a single element of the Project.

All this is simply a matter of original design and of Dam and Sluice Control. The currents likewise are always under perfect—if one wishes it, electric—regulation, through flood or drought. "Unimpeded navigation during all floods not exceeding 75,000 cubic feet per second" was claimed for the Project of 1901. Under this new Project even the 140,000 cubic feet per second of 1879 need not occasion a velocity of two and a half feet per second, because the waters are harnessed, and not let run wild.

WATER REQUIREMENTS.

The lockage water of the 90-foot six-lock Project of 1901 was estimated to require 35,127,960 cubic feet (1,000,000 meters cube) per day for "10 lockages equivalent to an annual traffic of 10,000,000 tons." This requirement is estimated to equal 406 cubic feet per second, Chagres flow. For two locks of 20 feet one may reckon $^2/_9$ of 409 or 91 cubic feet per second.

The lock-gate and sluice leakage, taking into account the diminished head, would be less than 50 per cent. but figured at 50 per cent. of the Commission's allowance of 250 c. f. one gets 125 second feet.

One may summarize, therefore, the water requirements as:

Lockage	91	c. f. per second	Chagres	Flow
Leakage	125	"	"	"	"	"
Contingencies	200	"	"	"	"	"
Evaporation	"207"	"	"	"	"	"
	623	"	"	"	"	"

This is about 60 per cent. of the water required by the Commission Plan of 1901. It is about the minimum of 600 c. f. s. recorded at Bohio besides which the new Lake Chagres has contributions below Bohio of at least 150 c. f. s. in the dryest seasons.

From the above it is evident that there need be anticipated no shortage of water under any circumstances, especially as Lakes Chagres and Panama and Pena Blanca are great reservoirs. It is certain therefore that though no water what ever were impounded by the River Dams at the outset of the dry season, there would yet be an ample natural supply.

CAPACITY OF BASINS, LAKES AND CHANNELS.

That of

Lake Chagres, per meter depth is	75,000,000 m³
Lake Panama " " " "	18,000,000 "
To the above one may add the storage capacity of the Pena Blanca Swamp Lake. This for its two meters depth is	3,400,000 "
Total	96,400,000 "

Discharge Capacity.	c. f. per second.
Chagres Lake Sluices	0 to 100,000
Panama " "	0 to 100,000
Cano Dam " "	0 to 5,000
Gamboa " "	0 to 100,000
Alhajuela Dam "	0 to 100,000

Under no conceivable circumstances, therefore, is it possible to have either too much or too little water.

OBISPO GATES.

This provision, made in order that the Culebra Section can be unwatered in case of exigency from great slides, is of doubtful utility to the +20 Project, but may be retained for any level above +40.

The foregoing gives a general idea of the salient features of the scheme. It is in order to direct attention to the changes of location inherent in it.

ALIGNMENT.

At Bohio the present curve may be modified. No other changes in alignment are now proposed, except the accepted new location from the 45 ft. sea-contour to the mouth of the Mindi River. The total curvature of the Canal is reduced somewhat below the 771° of the 1901 Plan

The length of the Canal between oceans will be 41½ miles exclusive of the submerged channels in Limon and Panama Bays.

It is possible that the Mindi and La Boca Lock sites, when definitely selected, may necessitate other slight changes in alignment.

ATLANTIC TERMINAL CITY.

The location through the Bay of Limon, made possible by the favorable borings lately reported, brings the Atlantic Terminal Harbor close to the present mouth of the Mindi River. The locks will be on the slopes of the Cerro Jaramillo (or Quebrancha) an eminence rising to a height of 375 feet, on whose more healthful site can be erected a new Colon.

On one side will be Lake Chagres, drowning the miasmic swamps, and below the locks will be disposed the Reception Basin, Coal Depot and Wharfs.

The Upper end of Limon Bay, enclosed by suitable concrete breakwaters, must be converted into a harbor of the first class with a wide and deep approach from the 45 ft. contour line. In view of the exposure of Limon Bay to Northers the alignment and position of the Breakwater Arms must be such as to completely protect the Canal Entrance and enable the Harbor area to absorb great waves just inside the Harbor Opening. In other words, the Arms of the Breakwater should leave not over a 700-ft. entrance. A mooted scheme to run the East Breakwater from Mindi Point and the Western one from Point Toro will permit waves to round their ends and make in the area, they are supposed to protect, a jumble dangerous to small craft and a nuisance to large vessels Colombo Harbor before the North Arm was built was a sufficient example of such a defect.

RETAINING BANKS.

Material excavated from the lock-site and its approaches, either side, will be utilized to make a very wide retaining bank 30 ft. high, connecting the hills which will, with the Barrage, create Lake Chagres. The Panama Railway embankment will require raising. Material for this is convenient at Monkey, Tiger and Lion Hills.

OUTLET DAM.

The site of the Outlet Dam is tentatively shown. It remains to be finally selected.

DAM AND BARRAGE SITES.

All the French and American Commissions are on record as stating that no dam-site exists below Bohio. Their conclusions were correct from the standpoint of a dam subjected to such highhead duty as their Projects imposed. Indeed, after another year of borings, whose results indicate less favorable conditions than formed the basis of the French and former Commission's designs, the present Commission and its corps of engineers deprecate the Bohio Dam and seem bent upon descending to the sea-level at any cost.

A low head Barrage can be put anywhere on the Chagres below the old Western Gatun Diversion, using principles of construction established by several illustrious examples, notably the one at Assiut in Egypt.

At Bohio a dam with a net head of 30 ft. is also practicable within a reasonable limit of cost. Reference will be made later to such a feature in connection with the Lake Chagres of this Project.

MAZANILLO BAY DIVERSION.

While it is practicable to turn the waters tributary to the East side of Lake Chagres into Mazanillo Bay, it will entail relatively little expense to allow them to enter Lake Chagres by suitable openings through the Panama Railway embankment.

UTILIZATION OF EXCAVATION.

MINDI TO LA BOCA.

From Mindi to La Boca in order to attain the 40-ft. channel depth, dredging will need to be carried only to —20 below mean sea level.

This insures the greatest possible utilization of the cuttings which were made by the French. The actual quantity remaining to be excavated may be readily estimated from recorded data, but these are not accessible.

Dredges can work and distribute hydraulicly, where material is suitable, from the +20-level cheaper and faster than from sea-level.

MINDI TO BOHIO.

As shown by Diagrams, nearly all of the canal excavation made by the French—about 20 to 22 million cubic yards—will be utilized. Of this the sea-level scheme can utilize only half.

BOHIO TO OBISPO.

The French excavated from this Section 12,350,000 cubic yards, of which probably over 11,000,000 c. y. will be utilized.

OBISPO TO THE PACIFIC.

All the excavations heretofore made here will be utilized. In the section between Pedro Miguel and La B·ca the new amount of excavation will be but a fraction of that hitherto contemplated. Much rock-work below sea-level will be eliminated.

EXCAVATION AT JUNCTION BASIN.

The sides of Junction Basin will be about 1150 feet long. The Chagres Entrance Channel and the outlet opening will be 400 to 500 feet broad at the water surface. Its basin will include about 20 acres.

BERM AND SPOILBANKS.

There are many lessons to be learned from the intimate knowledge of work ing conditions in a great canal like the Suez.

One of the most important is that the berms on either side should be very wide. The swift currents and eddies which invariably accompany the passage of a large vessel at a speed of only 3 or 4 knots per hour, continually undermine even firm earth. It has come to pass at Suez that now, no berm is left on either bank—and every underwater slope has been flattened by erosion and the operations of maintenance so that 1½ to 1 and 2 to 1 slopes have become from 2½ to 4 to 1.

The Suez Canal at its completion was supposed to have anticipated the need of centuries. Its sanguine eulogists ranked it among the enduring, finished products of that land of monuments. Yet, after a lapse of only thirty years its dimensions have proved so inadequate that the larger ships have ceased to essay it and are reaching Australia by the old weary route around the Cape

With the demand for enlargement pressing hard upon the dividends, the French regret now the short-sighted imminence of the spoilbanks and their high crest line.

Another most important precaution is to secure low, wide, spoilbanks instead of high, narrow ones. The crestline of a ship canal spoilbank should be always kept low—otherwise the expense of removing silt deposits, and of maintaining or deepening the cross section will be greatly enhanced.

Through Lakes Chagres and Panama especially it will be feasible and cheapest to spread the dredgings over very wide submerged spoil areas beyond a berm 100 feet or more wide, and this should be done.

GAMBOA AND ALHAJUELA DAMS AND BASINS.

Typical sections of these dams are shown on Plan No. II. Obviously similar dams can be put on each of the two main tributaries above the Alhajuela if it be deemed desirable to have larger catchment capacity. It will be noted that no heads are contemplated of the great heights required by the engineers of the other schemes.

These dam heights are:—

Bohio Project I, Bottom to Top, 165 +100 =265 ft.
Project II, Bottom to Top, 165 +78 =243 feet.
Project III, Bottom to Top, 165 +40 =205 feet.
Gamboa Project IV, Bottom to Top, 45 +155 =200 feet.
Project Bates, Bottom to Top, 45 + 92 =137 feet.
Alhajuela Project, Bates Bottom to Top, 62 + 92 = 154 feet.
Project Bates II, Bottom to Top, 62 + 171 = 233 feet. (*Comité Technique.*)

LAKE PANAMA.

This lake will be 20 feet above mean sea-level and 30 ft. above low water. The grade of the Panama Railway will need to be raised a few feet along the east and south shore of the Lake. All the swamps near the City will be submerged. The level of the Lake will be controlled by the Sluices of the Barrage.

LA BOCA BARRAGE.

The barrage will be thrown across the entrance to Rio Grande Bay above the La Boca Pier, connecting Sosoa Hill and the Hill West of the Mouth. This appears at first a venture, but it is one eminently feasible of design and execution on safe precedents. The sluice discharge will be on the west side of the center.

LA BOCA LOCK.

The Locks, on account of the expensive and valuable La Boca Pier, are placed above it near the axis of the present cutting instead of on the slope of either hill. The site must be coffer-dammed. While special provisions regarding foundations are required, the difficulties of safe construction are easily surmountable.

The present approach must be widened and deepened so as to present safe conditions to navigation at low tide. Provisions against constant silting occasioned by litoral drift ought to be part of the detailed plan.

PANAMA RAILWAY LINE DIVERSIONS.

Between San Pablo and Paraiso for 12½ miles the railway should be ultimately located on the east side of the Canal, although during the early stages of construction few changes will be required, except grade-raising at Lake Chagres and Lake Panama.

For this diversion it is probable that construction tracks can be utilized in part. A bridge may be essential between Obispo Basin and Gamboa Dam, as the crest of the dam should not be utilized.

ALTERNATIVES OR MODIFICATIONS OF LINDON BATES' PROJECT.

The foregoing constitutes an outline of the Project preferred by the author. Lakes Chagres and Panama would be formed if one fixed on levels anywhere from +25 to +7, although descent below plus 20 renders the lakes smaller in area and involves greatly increased quantities, which in turn increase cost of excavation and spoil distribution. If one fixed upon a level below +10 the Pacific Ocean could be impressed into service as the Feeding Reservoir. All lockage water necessary might be taken in during the last hour of the higher Spring tides.

One could therefore easily make a project for a practicable Mean Sea-Level Waterway with a combined Barrage and Lock near Miraflores, but the enormous amount of excavation required to construct a safe transit channel for the largest ships would run the cost to figures and to duration of execution which are practically prohibitory. Further, the time of transit of a large vessel in a sea-level canal would be longer than in this lock canal, because the vessels would have to proceed slowly and with much caution in a narrow channel for 41½ miles in the former; in the latter they would have 17¼ miles of free lake navigation and only 20¾ miles in a waterway, nowhere less than 8,000 sq. ft. in section. The currents of the north and south channels would offset each other, and several hours would be saved by reason of the open lake sections.

By making Dams, Lock and Spill near Bohio and a lock at Pedro Miguel in connection with Lakes Chagres and Panama, one may arrange a net head of only 30 ft at the former place.

This would give two levels, Lake Chagres from Mindi to Bohio at +20 ft. to 26 ft. Lake Bohio from Bohio to Pedro Miguel at +50 ft. to 52.5 ft. The length of the open lake navigation thus obtained may be increased to 30 miles. The quantities of excavation under this plan will be greatly diminished and the time of transit will be scarcely altered — as time lost at the new locks interposed, will be regained in passing through the extra 9 miles of lake.

The feeding of this higher summit level becomes a matter of vital moment, and it would be prudent to have reserve storage above Gamboa before the inset of dry seasons.

POWER AND LIGHT.

Electric Power can readily be provided for the service of the Canal, for its Terminal Cities, for its Public Utilities and Industries

Pilots, however, responsible for the safe transit of vessels at night will vastly prefer the system of placing a large searchlight on the stem of the ship, 20 ft. below their positions on the bridge, to any system of canal lighting which only blinds their vision.

During the construction period the writer does not advocate the use of electric power except for light and in shops. It will take too long to instal such a system, and few, if any, land-excavating machines are yet through the experimental stage in trying to use electric motors as prime movers.

Likewise he takes emphatic exception to the use of coal. In these tropics, coal burning requires too many laborers—men to unload vessels, to load and unload and transport cars, or barges, to load and unload wagons, to fire boilers, and to remove ashes.

Instead the writer proposed to instal an oil-pipe line from Colon to Panama with tanks and pumping stations, with branches to Alhajuela and to all points where fuel will be necessary.

SANITATION.

Lakes Chagres and Panama drowning the swamps adjacent to the Terminal Cities must have most beneficial effects upon the health of the engineering and construction forces, and upon the residents of the cities for all time. There will be no more wading in saturated stifling jungles, there will be much less vegetation, and the mosquito as a pest could be more easily controlled. In connection with the oil pipe line from which every breeding area can be reached the larvæ can be exterminated. The roads and embankments can likewise be relieved in good measure, by oil, from the plague of mud, which must so greatly handicap economies of construction.

DISPOSITION OF SILT AND CURRENTS.

The Chagres above Gamboa is a clear water, not a silt bearing stream. Provision, however, will be made to trap silt deposits above each dam. Accumulations above the Gamboa can be readily removed by using hopper dredges in the Obispo

Basin. The Obispo Basin is inherently a silt trap but this does not interfere with its navigation.

Deposits may be expected in the upper ends of Lake Chagres and Panama or Bohio, whence they are easily removed by hoppers.

In the Sea-Level Project there are no silt traps where removal operations can be centered. With very heavy flood making rains in the Chagres Valley below Gamboa, silt will be distributed for twenty-five miles along the bottom of the channel, necessitating more expensive removal. As the current debouching into the Atlantic Harbor may reach a high velocity much silt may be expected there also.

When a "norther" blows it piles the water up at high tide in the Bay of Limon, six feet above mean sea-level. Naturally, the water will back up, running rapidly to probably, beyond Culebra. Now should a flood rain fall in the watershed of the Canal below Gamboa, coincidently with the usual swift recession of the sea, there will be induced in the sea-level canal, for perhaps thirty miles, torrential currents, dangerously erosive, and detrimental to navigation.

Against such likely contingencies there is in the Sea-Level scheme no protection whatever. This phenomenon may be seen between Port Said and Lake Timsah in rainless, hurricane-free Egypt, where the writer has observed currents of 1.5 knots per hour due to on-shore winds. Only a few weeks ago the streets of Colon were under water owing to a "norther."

TURNING BASINS.

The Bates Projects provide several turning basins in the Lakes and at Obispo. Such facilities are desirable for both commercial and military needs.

TIMES OF TRANSIT.

The relation of the various projects to the time of transit can be observed in reviewing the actual steps incident to the passage of a ship through the Canal. The procedure would be that which has developed at Suez and which is, in general, as follows:

1st. The ship arriving at either terminal port would be brought to the mooring berth designated by the Harbor-Master.

2d. The Captain would go ashore with his ship papers, including his Canal-Tonnage certificate, and Canal officers would come aboard to verify these. Passengers, mail, express matter and freight, if any, would be landed at a wharf or by tender and lighters.

3d. The vessel would take on coal or stores if such were needed.

4th. Passengers, mail, etc., would embark.

5th. The Captain, having paid his dues and gotten his despatch order, would place the ship under the sailing direction of the appointed pilot. She would cast off and proceed through the Canal, getting despatch signals by flag or lights from stations every five or eight miles along the route.

6th. Arriving at the other terminal the pilot would be relieved. Passengers, mail, etc., would embark, the ship would receive her sailing orders and would leave for her Ocean journey.

It is thus inevitable that several hours are spent at the terminal ports. It is not unusual for a day to be consumed there.

If the locks are at the end of the Canal it follows therefore that time need not actually be lost in passing them, because the ship can make the transit during her necessary stay in port. The length of this stay at these end harbors will be the same whether the Canal be Sea-Level and tide-locked, or be terminal-locked.

If, on the other hand, the locks are in the Central reaches of the Canal, the time of passing through does count materially because it must include not simply the transit duration, but also the time for slowing down and for getting back to speed.

With these premises and explanations the following approximate table will show the duration of transit under the various projects.

TABLE.

SHOWING TIME OF TRANSIT FOR VARIOUS PROJECTS. FOR A VESSEL TYPE "D" 650X70X32 FT. REPORT 1901.

TIME	PROJECT		
	Sea Level.	Bates "A."	Bates "B."
Time without allowance for lockages and meetings . . . . , ...	9.96	7.08	5.87
Lockages	.71	.00	1.08
Meetings in Canal Sections	2.30	1.33	1 09
Meetings at locks or gates	.17	.00	.34
Total hours	13.14	8.41	8.98

The time of transit in the Commission Report of 1901 (+85) was estimated at 14.27 hours, which is approximately correct. For the +60 and +30 Projects the time will work out longer than for the Sea-Level scheme.

In actual experience therefore the time of transit is, under the Bates' Projects, from 4 to 5 hours shorter than under any of the proposed alternatives.

UNIT PRICES.

The several committees in estimating and comparing the probable costs of the various projects have, one and all, based their computations upon unit prices which they call identical for each proposed design, i. e.—the same unit prices were used in 1901 in comparing the total costs of Nicaragua and Panama and just lately in comparing the +60 and +30 and Sea-Level Schemes. The writer submits that this principle is radically and perniciously fallacious. The local conditions created and the methods of execution applicable to the different designs or Canal levels, have everything to do with varying the unit costs of construction. No two projects will work out at the same unit rates at Panama.

A schedule of unit prices identical for each instance, and some announced as a recent "revelation" from work extended over a month on the use of three of four new steam shovels, has been applied to the 60 ft., the 30 ft., and the Sea-Level estimates.

Consider a few axioms. A sea-level cut includes, for instance, an excavation in the section from Obispo to Miraflores of some 14,000,000 cubic yards below the high-tide plane. This excavation must necessarily be done "in the dry" by steam shovels, trains, etc. An item of allowance for pumping and lifting these and other tens of millions of tons from a vast saturated pit is surely in order. The material will not carry itself away on wings. It must be lifted mechanically and at great cost. But the steam-shovel schedule quite ignores such facts. The factors of lifting, pumping and transporting will be manifestly higher for the sea-level than for any other project.

Again, in the sea-level cut from Mindi to Tavernilla, some 30,000,000 or more cubic yards of earth are to be dredged and placed in adjacent spoil-banks This quantity weighs over 10 billion pounds. Each of these pounds has also to be lifted an average of 15 feet above water in order to be distributed. This, interpreted, gives 150 billion foot pounds of work. But it takes eight pounds of water to distribute one pound of material hydraulicly, hence the lift calls for 1,350 billion foot pounds of work. If, instead, the dredges operate on the +20 foot level nearly all of this vast extra work, entailing great waste of money, time and life, is obviated.

The same principle and facts hold through Lake Panama.

In any rational and searching analysis it becomes self-evident that the unit prices of excavation in the Lindon Bates Projects must work out lower than in any of the other projects And likewise that in the Sea-Level scheme they must be higher than in all the rest.

It is further incontrovertibly true that the fewest men by far and the least plant will be needed to execute the Lindon Bates designs, and contrariwise that the Sea-Level must demand, of all the plans, the greatest equipment, the largest labor force, the longest time, the highest cost in money and life, and the farthest future of deficits.

A further point concerns legislation. A Sea-Level scheme entails an additional large appropriation from Congress. Incidental to securing this, months must elapse and the whole subject of a canal be thrashed out anew in both House and

Senate.   The proposal of an added hundred million must turn men's minds back to Nicaragua with surmises if, perhaps, after all, that might not still prove the better route.   These pregnant questions have all been met, been discussed thoroughly and been settled well.   The legislation already secured and the appropriation heretofore considered adequate should be permitted to insure to the world this needed waterway.

ESTIMATES AND PROGRAM OF EXECUTION.

As much excavation as is practicable should be done with dredges working on the new lake levels, because these lakes enormously simplify all the problems of labor, of excavation, lift and distribution of spoil by floating plant.   This means that the lakes should be created as early as possible, together with the auxiliary works necessary for maintaining their levels and for regulating the Chagres.

The computations of quantities are possibly only under detailed plans, which full survey data must precede.   Manifestly, however, under either the +20 or the combined +20 and +50 Projects, the remaining excavation and works to be accomplished will cost materially less in time and money than under any other design which gives at all equal navigation facilities.   Comparison is challenged.

FINANCIAL ASPECTS FROM A GOVERNMENTAL STANDPOINT.

First under the heading of Primary Considerations the past analysis has embodied a forecast as to the probable outcome of the Canal enterprise considering the federal government as a business investor.   Government finance, however, does not ordinarily treat such matters from the standpoint of a corporation or of a business man.

Accordingly a supplementary analysis of the financial situation is here presented, dealing with the bearings of the several projects in line with what may be held to be a governmental attitude.

PANAMA RAILWAY.

This railroad property should belong wholly to the Government.   Both its stock and bonds should be all owned by the United States, and the present corporation should cease to exist.   As to its $3,000,000 of outstanding bonds, the Government has, in effect, now to pay very high interest charges.   Four and one-half per cent. and 6 per cent. interest is paid, while the Government can borrow all the money it may wish at but 2 per cent. per annum.   Until the policy of acquiring and retiring these bonds is adopted, one may consider that the road's commercial earnings take care of the interest and sinking fund required and other fixed and operating charges, and that no surplus is turned into the United States Treasury.   Such a course is reckoned in the following computations.

In a wide view, the terminals, equipment, track, etc., should be now improved so as to give the most efficient service to foreign, local and canal traffic, and the recent dividend might well have been applied to this purpose.

As the Government has made its internal canals and water highways free of tolls, so it might make the Panama Railway free to Coasting Trade between our Atlantic and Pacific seaboards and to export and import trade into Atlantic and Pacific ports carried in American vessels. Such a policy would vastly benefit the whole people and especially the American Marine, which needs it. It would be identical in principle with the assumption of Suez Canal dues by several European Governments. Suez dues work out about one dollar per ton weight, and this rate, with proper plant and equipment, would practically cover the actual cost of transferring cargoes across the Isthmus.

This principle applied at Panama would assure active competition and the carriage of canal supplies at low rates in American vessels.

TOLLS.

The fixing of future canal tolls at one dollar per net registered ton is believed to be wise. The Panama will be wider and deeper than the Suez; it will surely attract much Suez business and may force the improvement of the latter to similar dimensions. This would terminate the commercial monopoly which withholds the Orient from benefiting by having its commerce transported in the largest and most economical vessels which cannot utilize the Suez route. It makes no difference to the stockholders of the canal whether a vessel be loaded or light, and sums devoted to improvement would act to limit or reduce its present 26 per cent. dividend.

The Suez Canal, permitting a draft of only 27 feet 5 inches, continues a real bar to the best navigation, and fails to serve the highest economic interests of Europe and the East. It will be ultimately obliged to deepen and widen its waterway and reduce its tolls, remaining always, however, one of the finest commercial investments in the world.

COMPARATIVE FINANCIAL OUTLOOK FOR AUTHORIZED AND SEA-LEVEL PROJECT.

Congress has authorized the issue of $130,000,000 in bonds for the Panama Canal. The recommendations of the Committee for a sea-level canal estimates a construction expenditure of $230,500,000, which, as per schedule, will require the authorization of $85,500,000 bonds additional, or a total of $215,500,000 These sums represent the bonded indebtedness for two projects of the undertaking.

33

Project.	Appropriation for zone purchase.	Appropriation for canal purchase.	Appropriation for use prior to bond issue	Bonds authorized or required.	Unappropriated.
1901	10,000,000	40,000,000	10,000,000	130,000,000	5,000,000
+60	10,000,000	40,000,000	10,000,000	163,013,000	5,000,000
+30	10,000,000	40,000,000	10,000,000	179,213,000	5,000,000
S-level	10,000,000	40,000,000	10,000,000	215,500,000	5,000,000

It is to be assumed that all other expenditures, such as the $50,000,000 already paid for Panama Canal Co.'s interest and for the zone strip and what will have to be paid out in future for interest on bonds issued during the construction period, for purchase of Panama Railway Bonds, etc., is to come out of the Treasury, and against which no interest charges will be considered.

The fixed charges of the undertaking become the interest on the bonds issued as above described, plus the operation costs which have been stated at $2,000,000, and which will be figured the same for any project.

With the Irrigation Act as a precedent, it is assumed that the United States Treasury will provide funds for starting the exploitation, will meet all deficits (such as will result from the first and second year of operation) and will receive all surplus above operating expenses, debiting and crediting the same to the Canal account without any interest charges whatever.

The following method is assumed for purposes of comparing the results of the authorized canal and the sea-level project, along the lines described.

Referring to the diagram:

a—The deficits would be paid.

b—The first surplus earning would be applied to refunding the cumulated deficits.

c—The surplus earnings after the deficits are made good would be applied to a Reserve Working Fund of $10,000,000.

d—The surplus earnings after the above fund is complete would be applied in any manner prescribed by Congress, but always with the provision that any draft on the Working Reserve Fund due to contingencies or new construction shall be restored before the surplus is used for any other purpose.

With the above premises the estimates which are embodied in the diagram work out to the following results:

34

YEARS	AUTHORIZED CANAL $130,000,000 BOND ISSUE			FOR BOTH PROJECTS	SEA-LEVEL PROJECT $215,500,000 BOND ISSUE		
	Remarks	Difference.	Expenses.	Income.	Expense.	Difference.	Remarks.
1915	Deficit	$3,600,000	$4,600,000	$1,000,000	$6,310,000	$5,310,000	Deficit
1916	Surplus	400,000	4,600,000	5,000,000	6,310,000	1,310,000	Deficit
1917	Surplus	2,679,000	4,600,000	7,279,000	6,310,000	969,000	Surplus
1918	Surplus	3,006,600	4,600,000	7,606,600	6,310,000	1,296,600	Surplus
1919	Surplus	3,334,200	4,600,000	7,934,200	6,310,000	1,624,200	Surplus
1920	Surplus	3,661,800	4,600,000	8,261,800	6,310,000	1,951,800	Surplus
1921	Surplus	3,989,400	4,600,000	8,589,400	6,310,000	2,279,400	Surplus
1922	Surplus	4,317,000	4,600,000	8,917,000	6,310,000	2,607,000	Surplus
1923	Surplus	4,644,600	4,600,000	9,244,600	6,310,000	2,934,600	Surplus
1924	Surplus	4,971,200	4,600,000	9,571,200	6,310,000	3,261,200	Surplus
1925	Surplus	5,298,800	4,600,000	9,898,800	6,310,000	3,588,800	Surplus
1926	Surplus	5,626,400	4,600,000	10,226,400	6,310,000	3,916,400	Surplus
1927	Surplus	5,954,000	4,600,000	10,554,000	6,310,000	4,244,000	Surplus

REMARKS	Authorised Canal.	Sea-Level Project
Total Deficit...................................	$3,600,000	$6,520,000
Total Deficit Refunded in.........................	1917–1918	1920–1921
$10,000,000 Reserve complete in...................	1920–1921	1923–1924
Available accumulated surplus end 1927.............	$34,283,000	$12,053,000

NOTE: No contingencies or extra expenditures which would involve drafts on the reserve working fund have been considered.

The foregoing calculations do not consider interest on bonds issued during the construction period of ten years, which may be for the authorized Canal $13,000,000 and for the Sea-Level scheme $21,550,000.

This exhibit confirms the fact that from the standpoint of government financing, as well as from a business view, the canal should cost no more than the amount already authorized by Congress.

SUMMARY
OF
ELEMENTS OF BATES' PROJECTS.

PROJECT A.

1. Atlantic Harbor Approach.

2. Atlantic Harbor Breakwaters.

3. Atlantic Harbor Excavation and Reclamation.

4.   Lake Chagres.
5.   Lake and Railway Embankments.
6.   Atlantic Locks.
7.   Chagres Barrage.
8.   Pena Blanca Lake, Embankment, Spillway.
9.   Rio Cano Dam.
10.   Canal Waterway with Expanding Section from Obispo to Lake Chagres.
11.   Obispo Basin.
13.   Miscellaneous small watershed works adjacent to Canal, between Lakes Chagres and Panama.
14   Lake Panama.
15.   Pacific Lock
16.   Pacific Barrage and Discharge Channel.
17.   La Boca Approach.
18.   Gamboa Dam and Basin.
19.   Alhajuela Dam and Basin.

PROJECT B.

1.   Atlantic Harbor Approach.
2.   Atlantic Harbor Breakwaters.
3.   Atlantic Harbor Excavation and Reclamation.
4.   Lake Chagres.
5.   Lake and Railway Embankments.
6.   Atlantic Locks.
7.   Chagres Barrage.
8   Pena Blanca Lake, Embankment, Spillway
9.   Lake Behio and Dam.
10.   Gigante Spillway.
11.   Obispo Basin.
12   Canal, Obispo Basin to Pedro Miguel Locks and Spillway sluices
13   Obispo Gate.
14   Lake Panama.
15   Pacific Lock
16   Pacific Barrage and Discharge Channel
17   La Boca Approach
18   Alhajuela or Gamboa Lake.
19   Alhajuela or Gamboa Dam.

SPECIAL FEATURES.

PROJECT A.

Of the elements summarized further remarks are added as to the character and duty of the works numbered 5, 6, 7, 9, 15, 16, 18 and 19.

5. *Chagres Lake Embankments*. If these embankments are given ample width, volume and height, and are provided with rip-rapped slopes where they are exposed to wave motion, and sheet piling be driven which will form a septum to prevent underflow, there can be no possible danger of failure. The banks may be built cheapest by combined train and hydraulic-dredge operations. The head of water is small and the lake is without currents. The levee will be much more substantial and more safe than that for instance which protects New Orleans.

6. *Atlantic Locks*. The only question possible in regard to these works relates to the foundation which may or may not be upon rock. It is altogether probable that at Mindi, on the slopes of Jaramillo Hill, or at Gatum, a rock site is available. But the architectural art of making foundations is unquestionably equal to providing a solid and immovable base for this work even in earth.

7 *and* 16. *Chagres and Pacific Barrages*. These low head, Insubmergible Under Sluice Barrages present conditions which are completely paralleled in far greater works in Egypt. If the foundations are simply earth we have only to look to the Assiut Barrage; if rock, to the Assuan Dam. The Pacific Barrage may be on the slopes of West Rio Grande Hill. There are no unsolved problems here.

9, 18 *and* 19. The Regulating Dams are founded on rock, and in height, in head and in form they are substantially the same as the Assuan Dam. The dams and barrages may be designed in masonry, "béton armèe" or "ribbed concrete" to suit local conditions. Their sluices have to deal with but a tithe of the flood waters of the Nile. There are no experiments here.

15. *Pacific Lock*. Firm earth or rock sites are to be found on the lower slopes of Sosoa or West Rio Grande Hills at La Boca; but, because of the location of the La Boca Railway Pier, it is best to consider first a site above, where positive data as to the character of the formation are not accessible. If it be unfavorable, a plan which conserves La Boca Pier for some useful purpose and permits the Lock to be located on the west slope of Sosoa Hill should be adopted. La Boca Pier would make an excellent and needed coal station if equipped with modern appliances, or it could be converted into a naval depot. Its present use can, in any case, continue during the construction period.

9 and 10. *Lake Bohio and Dam and Gigantè Spillway:* The Project of the Comitè Technique may be intervened in Project A, the Lakes Chagres and Panama being raised to 22.5, and the Lake Bohio level fixed at their minimum of 52.5.

This reduces the net head of Bohio lake to 30 feet, greatly simplifying all the problems presented by the formation disclosed at the Dam-Site. A core-earth dam becomes free from hazard. Seepage and percolation are minimized.

10 *and* 12. *Pedro Miguel and Gigantè Spillway.* In this project the French plan may be adopted. It becomes also feasible and desirable to provide a Diversion and Sluice-Way in connection with--but to the west side of—the Pedro Miguel Lock, to feed Lake Panama and to act as an extra run off. None of these works present any construction difficulties. The flow from the Gigantè Spillway into Lake Chagres becomes harmless. It will not overhang the Canal in a rushing torrent, as it must under either the Commission Plan of 1901 or that of the Comité Technique.

The inevitable conclusion is that as to Project A there can be no reasonable objection, and as to Project B, with its 26 miles of lake navigation, reduced quantities of excavation and reduced net head in Lake Bohio, there is far less ground for criticism than must attach to each and all of the Projects I, II, III, or IV heretofore considered.

Tunnels. While one or more tunnels can, presumably, be run from either the Gamboa or Alhajuela Basins, they are unnecessary and are unjustified except as an academic increase in the factors of safety incorporated in the Undersluices of the Dams.

In the Nile valley, 500 miles above Cairo, where the rugged hills have closed in to bar the desert, a dam has been built. Below it stretches to the far sea the Old World granary, the land whose soil has been a treasury. The destruction of this dam would project upon Egypt a catastrophe unparalleled in all history. Johnstown extended to a nation; Atlantis engulfed in an hour—such would be the tale that would appall all after ages. But under this dam, holding back its 36,000,000,000 cubic feet of river, the Nile people are as safe and untroubled as though it were their very granite hills. Through its gates come measured and controlled the fertilizing waters, and nine millions of Egyptians live under the warrant of the Assuan Dam.

In the experience of its success no further word is needed in defense of the safety of a project incorporating not a full but an empty-basin principle for its central feature.

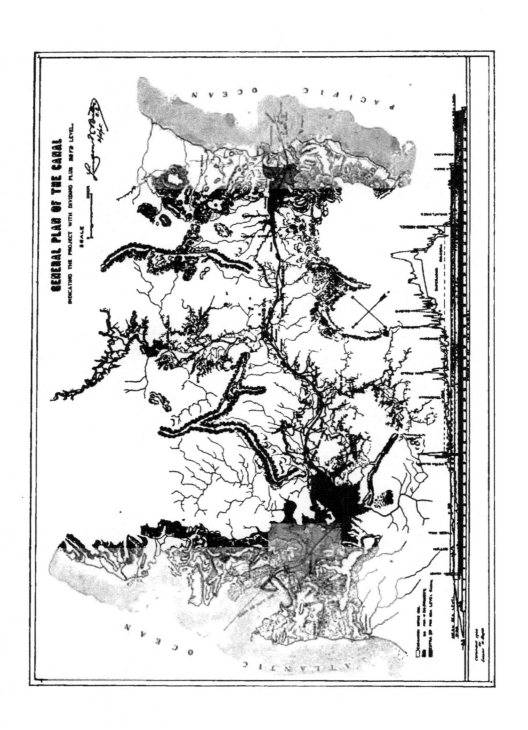

GENERAL PLAN OF THE CANAL

INDICATING THE PROJECT WITH DIVIDING PLAN 84/72 LEVEL.

SCALE

PACIFIC OCEAN

ATLANTIC OCEAN

GENERAL PLAN OF THE CANAL

INDICATING THE PROJECT WITH DIVIDING PLUS SEA LEVEL

SCALE

PACIFIC OCEAN

PROJECT FOR PANAMA CANAL.
Types of Dam and Barrage, Plate III.

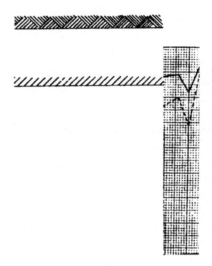

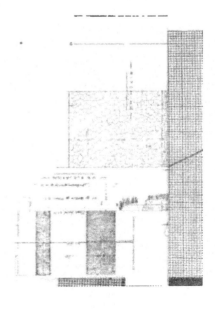

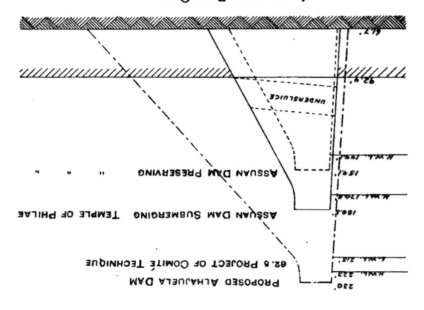

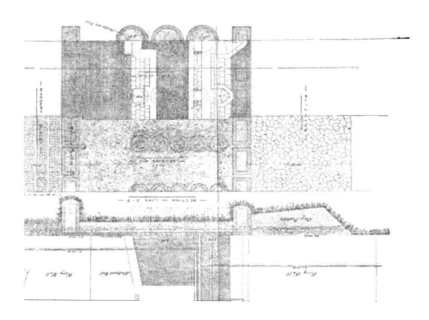

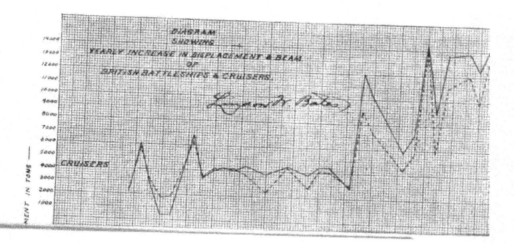

DIAGRAM
SHOWING
YEARLY INCREASE IN DISPLACEMENT & BEAM
OF
BRITISH BATTLESHIPS & CRUISERS.

CRUISERS

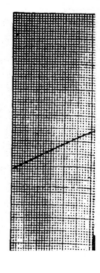

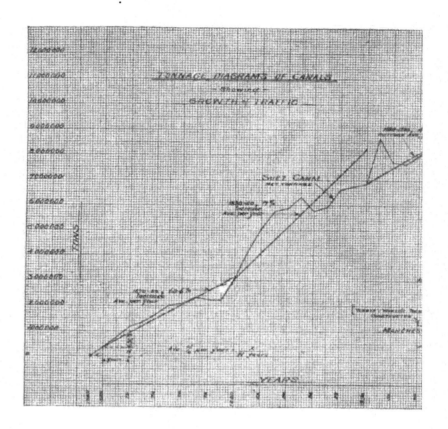

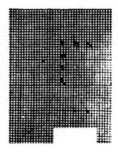

CPSIA information can be obtained at www.ICGtesting.com
Printed in the USA
BVOW09s1049010515

398583BV00013B/127/P

9 781146 043069